ANIMAL LIVES

Fish

WORLD
BOOK

a Scott Fetzer company
Chicago
www.worldbook.com

World Book, Inc.
233 N. Michigan Avenue
Chicago, IL 60601
U.S.A.

For information about other World Book publications, visit our Web site at **http://www.worldbook.com** or call **1-800-WORLDBK (967-5325).**

For information about sales to schools and libraries, call **1-800-975-3250 (United States),** or **1-800-837-5365 (Canada).**

Editorial:

Editor in Chief: Paul A. Kobasa
Project Manager: Cassie Mayer
Writer: Daniel Kenis
Researcher: Jacqueline Jasek
Manager, Contracts & Compliance
 (Rights & Permissions): Loranne K. Shields
Indexer: David Pofelski

Graphics and Design:

Manager: Tom Evans
Coordinator, Design Development
 and Production: Brenda B. Tropinski
Book design by: Don Di Sante
Senior Cartographer: John Rejba

Pre-Press and Manufacturing:

Director: Carma Fazio
Manufacturing Manager: Steven K. Hueppchen
Senior Production Manager: Jan Rossing

Library of Congress Cataloging-in-Publication Data

Fish / World Book.
 p. cm. -- (Animal lives)
 Includes index.
 Summary: "An introduction to fish and their physical characteristics, life cycle, behaviors, and adaptations to various underwater habitats. Features include maps, diagrams, fun facts, glossary, resource list, and index"--Provided by publisher.
 ISBN 978-0-7166-0404-4
 1. Fishes--Juvenile literature. I. World Book, Inc.
 QL617.2.F48 2009
 597--dc22
                 2009008534

Picture Acknowledgments:

Front Cover: © Specta/Shutterstock; Back Cover: © Kristian Sekulic, Shutterstock

© Alaska Stock/Alamy Images 24; © blickwinkel/Alamy Images 12; © Mark Boulton, Alamy Images 15; © Brandon Cole Marine Photography/Alamy Images 13; © Phil Degginger, Alamy Images 36; © David Fleetham, Alamy Images 22; © Legge/Alamy Images 42; © MIXA/Alamy Images 40; © Michael Patrick O'Neill, Alamy Images 30; © James D. Watt, Stephen Frink Collection/Alamy Images 16; © Maximilian Weinzierl, Alamy Images 29; © Bernard Photo Productions/Animals Animals 7; © Breck P. Kent, Animals Animals 39; AP/Wide World 41; © Brandon Cole Marine Photography 13; © Fred Bavendam, Minden Pictures 10; © Stephen Dalton, Minden Pictures 16; © Hans Leijnse, Minden Pictures 25; © Michael Quinton, Minden Pictures 4; © Atsushi Sakurai, Minden Pictures 22; © Becca Saunders, Minden Pictures 31; © Norbert Wu, Minden Pictures 26; © Chelsea Baker, Naples Zoo at Caribbean Gardens 37; © James L. Amos, National Geographic Stock 12; © Bill Curtsinger, National Geographic Stock 11; © George Grall, National Geographic Stock 9; © Norbert Wu, Minden Pictures/National Geographic Stock 17; © Paul Nicklen, National Geographic Stock 38; © Brian J. Skerry, National Geographic Stock 10; © Jane Burton, Nature Picture Library 23; © Georgette Douwma, Nature Picture Library 4; © Hugh Maynard, Nature Picture Library 38; © Jose B. Ruiz, Nature Picture Library 42; © Kim Taylor, Nature Picture Library 37; © Jeffrey Rotman, Biosphoto/Peter Arnold, Inc. 40; © Bob Evans from Peter Arnold, Inc. 28; © Doug Perrine from Peter Arnold, Inc. 43; © Jonathan Bird, SeaPics.com 21, 28; © Mark Conlin, SeaPics.com 30, 33, 35; © Matthew J. D'Avella, SeaPics.com 34; © Reinhard Dirscherl, SeaPics.com 18; © Hideyuki Utsunomiya, e-Photography/SeaPics.com 33; © David B. Fleetham, SeaPics.com 19; © Rodger Klein, SeaPics.com 15; © Michael Patrick O'Neill, SeaPics.com 31; © Doug Perrine, SeaPics.com 20, 27, 29; © D. R. Schrichte, SeaPics.com 14; © Andre Seale, SeaPics.com 26; © Patrice Ceisel, Shedd Aquarium/SeaPics.com 39; © Edward G. Lines, Shedd Aquarium/SeaPics.com 8; © James D. Watte, SeaPics.com 14, 20; © Norbert Wu, Minden Pictures 34; © Shutterstock 6, 7, 9, 18, 19, 32, 44, 45; © National Geographic/SuperStock 5; © Pacific Stock/SuperStock 32.

All maps and illustrations are the exclusive property of World Book, Inc.

Animal Lives
Set ISBN: 978-0-7166-0401-3

Printed in China by:
Shenzhen Donnelley Printing Co., Ltd,
Guangdong Province
3rd Printing August 2013

Table of Contents

There is a glossary of terms on page 46. Terms defined in the glossary are in type **that looks like this** on their first appearance on any spread (two facing pages).

What Are Fish?

Fish are animals that live in water. Fish come in an amazing variety of shapes and sizes. Some fish look like wriggling worms. Others look like pancakes. Some fish can blow themselves up like balloons. A few kinds of fish have huge mouths that can swallow things twice their size!

Fish come in many colors. Some have bright stripes or polka dots. Many fish blend in with their surroundings so well that you can barely see them.

Many fish have bright colors. These two butterflyfish swim against a group of bannerfish.

What makes a fish?

All the different kinds of fish have some things in common. They are all **vertebrates.** This means they have a backbone, just like you. They breathe with body parts called **gills.** In addition, almost all fish are **cold-blooded.** Their bodies stay the same temperature as the water around them.

Some animals, like starfish and jellyfish, have "fish" in their names. But these animals are not real fish because they do not have backbones.

The world of fish

The underwater world is very different from life on land. It is also just as varied as land. The surface of the

Trout, like almost all fish, are cold-blooded. They stay the same temperature as the water.

Fun Fact

There are almost 25,000 different kinds of fish. That is more than all the other kinds of vertebrates put together!

ocean is sunlit. But the bottom of the ocean is pitch-black. In the deepest ocean, the pressure is so great that a human being would get crushed.

Oceans are filled with salty water. But lakes, rivers, and streams have fresh water (water that is not salty).

Fish can live in all of these underwater places. Some fish can even come out of the water and live on dry land!

Fish live almost anywhere there is water. These snappers swim among underwater mangrove roots.

What Are Features of Fish?

The bodies of fish have a number of **adaptations**. Adaptations are features that help a living thing survive in the place where it lives.

All fish have certain features in common, such as tails and fins.

Super swimmers

Most fish are well adapted for swimming. Their bodies are usually smoothly shaped, so they easily glide through the water.

Fish swim by moving fanlike parts of their body called fins. They also have a dorsal fin on their back. The dorsal fin helps keep them upright.

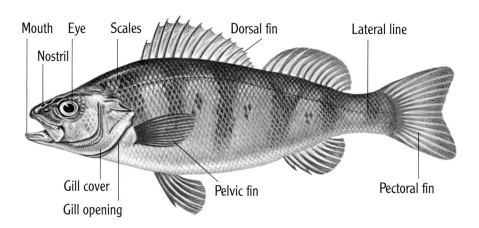

Mouth | Eye | Scales | Dorsal fin | Lateral line
Nostril
Gill cover
Gill opening
Pelvic fin
Pectoral fin

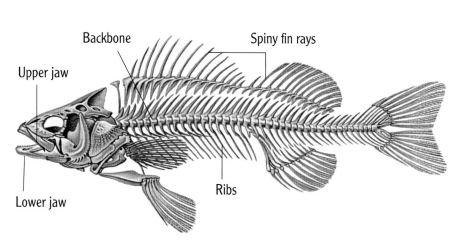

Backbone | Spiny fin rays
Upper jaw
Lower jaw
Ribs

Fish use fins to swim in the water. They also have backbones—just like you do.

Breathing underwater

Human beings have to hold their breath when they go underwater. That is because we breathe air with lungs. But fish can breathe just fine in the water. They use their **gills** to breathe.

Some animals, like dolphins and whales, look a lot like fish. But they breathe with lungs, just like people. They have to come up to the water's surface to breathe.

Tough fish

Most fish have scales. The scales act like armor, protecting their bodies. Fish also have tough, slippery skin. The skin is slippery because it produces mucus—the same slimy stuff that's in your nose.

Fish usually eat other animals. Almost all fish have mouths with jaws. They use their jaws to bite and eat food. But a few fish do not have jaws. Their mouths are round and cannot be closed for biting.

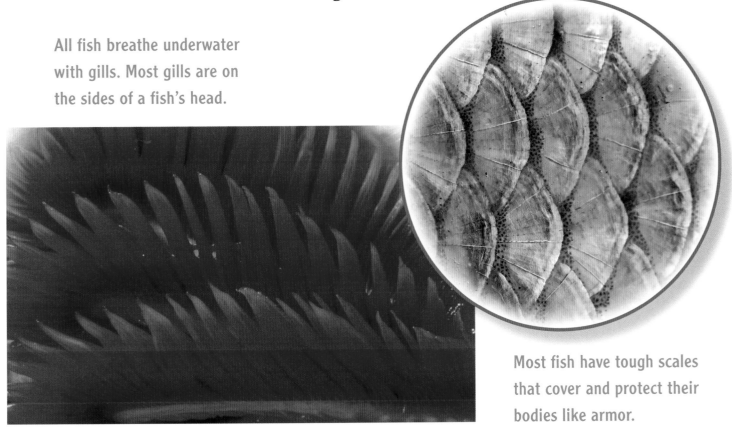

All fish breathe underwater with gills. Most gills are on the sides of a fish's head.

Most fish have tough scales that cover and protect their bodies like armor.

What Do Most Fish Have in Common?

Most fish have a skeleton made out of hard bone. Scientists group these fish together as bony fish. There are many different **species** (kinds) of bony fish. They all have certain features in common.

Creature features

All bony fish have jaws, and most have teeth. In addition, all bony fish have a **swim bladder**. The swim bladder is a body part that can fill with gas like a balloon. It lets the fish float in the water.

Bony fish have swim bladders that allow them to float.

Swim bladder

Seahorses look different from most fish but they have the same kind of bony skeleton.

The snakelike moray eel is a bony fish. It can slither into tight holes to hide.

Most fish have tall, bony fins that help them swim.

Spiny fins

Most bony fish have spiny fins made of bone. The spines give the fins their shape. Familiar fish like catfish and tuna have spiny fins. So do strange-looking fish, like eels and seahorses.

Spiny fins come in many different shapes. This is because fish have **adapted** to their environments in many different ways. Flyingfish have winglike spiny fins. They use them to glide above the water's surface. The mudskipper has muscular fins. It uses them to hop around on land.

A few kinds of bony fish have fleshy fins. They are related to fish that lived millions of years ago.

Are Sharks and Rays Fish?

Sharks and rays are fish that have several unique features. Unlike bony fish, sharks and rays have skeletons that are made of rubbery **cartilage.** Cartilage is softer than bone.

The whale shark is the largest fish of all. It only eats tiny animals.

Body armor

Sharks and most rays also have skin that is covered by toothlike scales and feels like sandpaper. These rough scales are like a suit of armor that protects the fish from enemies.

Sharks

Sharks live throughout the world's oceans. Most sharks have round, torpedo-shaped bodies that can move quickly through the water.

Sharks come in all sizes. The largest shark—and the largest of all fish—is the whale shark. It grows up to 40 feet (12 meters) long and weighs more than two

Hammerhead sharks are fierce hunters. Their wide-spaced eyes and nostrils help them search for food.

elephants! But the whale shark is not dangerous to people. It only eats tiny animals near the surface of the water. Some sharks eat bigger animals like large fish and other sharks.

Sharks have many **adaptations** that make them great hunters. They have rows of razor-sharp teeth that they lose and regrow throughout their lives. They also have an excellent sense of smell.

Rays

Rays are related to sharks, but they don't look much like them. Most rays have flattened, pancake-shaped bodies. They use their large, winglike fins to swim through the water or to bury themselves into the sand to hide. Some rays have poisonous stingers on their tails.

Most rays swim along the bottom of the ocean, where they feed on clams, shellfish, small fish, and other creatures. The huge manta ray swims along the surface. Like the whale shark, it only eats tiny animals there.

Stingrays have flattened bodies and poisonous stingers on their tails. They usually swim along the ocean floor.

What Fish Are Like Living Fossils?

More than 350 million years ago, wormlike fishes slithered through the dark waters near the ocean floor. They didn't look like most fish today. They didn't have jaws and scales, and their mouths were shaped like circles or slits. These fish, called lampreys and hagfish, are still around today. They give us a glimpse of what fish were like long ago.

Lampreys hook onto other fish with their round mouths and suck their blood.

Creature features

Like sharks, lampreys and hagfish have skeletons made out of rubbery **cartilage**. But unlike sharks, their bodies are slimy and scaleless, and they do not have jaws. In a way, lampreys and hagfish look more like big worms than fish.

Lamprey

Hagfish are scavengers. They usually eat dead animals they find on the sea floor.

Lampreys

A lamprey is kind of like a huge leech. Its round mouth is filled with teeth. Some lampreys use these teeth to hook onto the flesh of other fish. Since lampreys have no jaws, they cannot bite. But their mouths work like suction cups.

A lamprey's tongue is sharp and works like a knife. Once attached to a fish, a lamprey uses its tongue to cut into the fish's flesh. Then the lamprey sucks blood and other fluids through the cut.

Lampreys live in both fresh water and the ocean. Ocean lampreys can grow 3 feet (91 centimeters) long.

Hagfish

Hagfish are much like lampreys, but they are almost completely blind and have a slitlike mouth instead of a round one. Hagfish use their sharp teeth to eat dead or dying animals. They usually eat dead animals from the inside out!

Fun Fact

Hagfish are some of the slimiest of all animals. An Atlantic hagfish can make enough slime in one minute to fill a bucket!

What Senses Do Fish Have?

Fish have the same senses that you do. They can see, hear, smell, taste, and touch. But fish also have special **adaptations** that help them sense underwater.

This half-buried Pacific halibut has both of its eyes on one side of its head.

Fish eyes

Most fish have eyes on either side of the head. This arrangement lets them see to the right and to the left at the same time.

Some fish have strange eyes. The adult flatfish has both eyes on one side of its head. It spends its time on the ocean floor, so it only needs to look in one direction—up.

The anableps fish looks like it has four eyes. But its eyes are actually made up of two different parts. The fish swims right at the surface of the water. The top parts of its eyes see out above the surface of the water. The bottom parts see underwater.

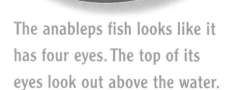

The anableps fish looks like it has four eyes. The top of its eyes look out above the water.

Sensing the water

Most fish have a special sense system that other animals do not have. This system is called the **lateral line.** It is a system of tubelike channels underneath the skin. Water flows into these channels.

A fish uses its lateral line system to sense changes in the movement of water. If you tried to sneak up on a fish from behind, it could still sense you. Its lateral line system would "feel" the movements you made in the water.

Fun Fact

Catfish and sturgeon are fish that have whiskerlike growths by their mouths. These growths help them taste and touch.

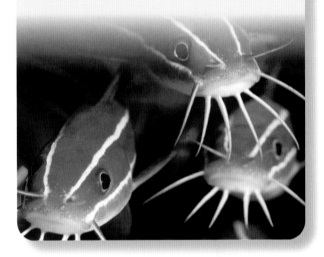

The lateral line runs down the sides of a fish's body. It helps fish sense changes in the movement of water.

Lateral line

How Do Fish Hunt?

A few kinds of fish eat plants, or plantlike **algae.** Some other fish eat dead animals they find. But most fish catch and eat live animals, including other fish. These fish have many **adaptations** that help them hunt in the water.

Mighty mouths

Fish have mouths made for hunting and eating. Most fish have jaws that can chomp down on food. Razor-sharp teeth line the mouths of fish like sharks and piranhas (*pih RAHN yuhs*).

Some fish have strangely shaped mouths. Swordfish have long, beaklike jaws they use to slash or spear **prey** (hunted animals).

Lampreys do not have jaws at all. Their mouths are like round suckers. Some lampreys use their mouths to attach themselves to other fish. Then they slash open the fish's skin with their sharp tongue. They feed on the blood from the wound.

The archerfish spits water at insects above the surface. This knocks them down into the water so the fish can eat them!

Weapons and traps

Some fish have special abilities that help them hunt. Electric eels can create electric shocks that stun their prey. Archerfish shoot streams of water at insects resting above the water's surface. This knocks the insect down into the water, where the archerfish can grab it.

Deep below the ocean, the water is pitch-black. But a deep-sea fish called the anglerfish has a body part that glows in the dark. This body part dangles right in front of their huge, fang-filled mouth. Its glowing light lures fish and other animals close. Then the anglerfish swallows them up.

The anglerfish lures smaller fish close to its mouth with a dangling, glowing body part.

How Do Fish Escape?

Human beings have it easy. They rarely have to worry about a bigger animal gobbling them up in a single bite. But most fish are always in danger of being eaten by **predators** (animals that hunt). Fish have a number of **adaptations** that can save them from ending up in a bigger fish's stomach.

Clownfish hide in the tentacles of sea anemones. The stinging tentacles hurt other fish.

Clever camouflage

Many fish are colored dark on top and light on their bellies. This coloring works to **camouflage,** or hide, the fish. If you look up at such a fish, its light belly looks like the bright surface waters. If you look down at the fish, its top is dark like the deep waters below. No matter which direction you look at the fish from, it blends in with its surroundings.

Some fish have camouflage that makes them look like they aren't fish at all. The poisonous stonefish looks like a rock. Pipefish look like long, skinny weeds. The leafy seadragon could easily be mistaken for a floating piece of seaweed.

The scorpionfish blends in with rocky sea floors. It is also very poisonous.

Escape artists

Most fish can quickly swim away from predators. Flyingfish and needlefish can jump out of the water to escape. Eels dig holes and hide in them.

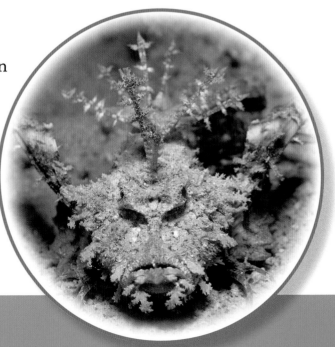

Clownfish have a special hiding place. They live in sea anemones—animals that look like flowering plants. A sea anemone has stinging tentacles (feelers) that hurt other kinds of fish. But clownfish have adapted protection from the stings.

Sharp-tasting fish

Some fish have sharp spikes that protect them. The spikes of scorpionfish, stonefish, and stingrays are poisonous. They can harm or kill other fish that try to eat them.

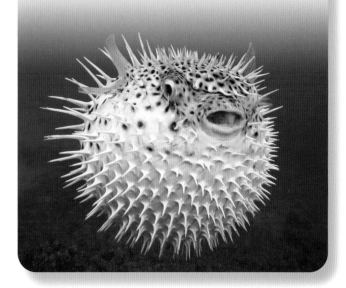

Predators have trouble spotting leafy seadragons. They look like drifting bits of seaweed.

Do Fish Live in Groups?

Some fish live by themselves. But other fish swim together in groups called **schools.** Schools of fish swim together like a single body.

The fish in a school swim in the same direction, at the same speed.

School size

The number of fish in a school can depend on the **species** of fish. A school of tuna may have about 25 fish. A school of herring has millions of fish!

All the fish in a school are about the same size. Baby fish and adult fish are never in the same school. Some fish join a school when they are young and stay with it their entire lives.

Schools of fish have many pairs of eyes. They spot food faster than a single fish can.

Why stay in schools?

Fish form schools for a number of reasons. One fish swimming alone makes an easy meal for **predators.** But a big group of fish can help protect individual members of the school.

Schools also make it easier for fish to find food. Thousands of fish looking for food have a better chance of finding it than a single fish does.

Some fish do not stay in a school all the time. They form schools only when they eat, rest, or lay eggs. Other fish stay in a school only when they are young.

All the fish in a school are about the same age and size.

How Do Fish Grow?

All fish go through similar stages of development, from the time they hatch from an egg to the time they grow into adult fish. Together, these stages make up a fish's **life cycle.**

Eggs start developing into fish after they are fertilized by an adult male fish.

Eggs

Fish start their life as an egg. Female fish lay eggs in the water. Some lay thousands or even millions of eggs at once!

Once the eggs are laid, they have to be **fertilized** by a male fish. Only then can the eggs grow into fish. But most eggs never become adult fish. They are eaten by **predators** or swept away in currents.

Some fish leave their eggs once they lay them. Others protect their fertilized eggs. Female salmon cover the eggs with gravel. A male jawfish holds the eggs in his mouth, guarding them from predators. The male smallmouth bass will fight anything that comes near the eggs after they are hatched.

A male jawfish holds his eggs in his big mouth to protect them from predators.

Larvae

After a fish egg hatches, it is called a **larva.** Two or more eggs are called larvae.

Larvae are like baby fish, but some larvae do not look much like adult fish. Certain larvae hatch with a sac of egg yolk still attached. The yolk provides them with food before their mouth and stomach start to work.

Larvae grow into adult fish after a certain amount of time. Some small kinds of fish larvae take only minutes to become adults. Other kinds take months. A fish is an adult when it can lay or fertilize eggs of its own. Most fish continue to grow as adults.

Some fish, like seahorses and salmon, live for only a few years. Others, like some **species** of pike, can live up to 70 years!

Fun Fact Male seahorses hold fertilized eggs in a pouch. When the eggs hatch, the seahorse larvae shoot out of the pouch.

Some fish, like the female African mouthbrooder, guard their young.

Do Fish Migrate?

Some fish travel long distances to lay eggs. These travels are called **migrations.** Fish migrations can be amazing and dangerous journeys.

Salmon migrate from the ocean into freshwater rivers. They swim long distances against fast-flowing currents.

Freshwater and saltwater migrations

Water in lakes and rivers is fresh water. It is not salty. But the water of the ocean is quite salty. Because of this difference in saltiness, only a few fish can travel between the ocean and fresh water.

Salmon are one such kind of fish. Adult salmon migrate from the ocean into rivers to lay their eggs. They have to swim upstream against swift flowing water. Some salmon swim 2,000 miles (3,200 kilometers) upstream!

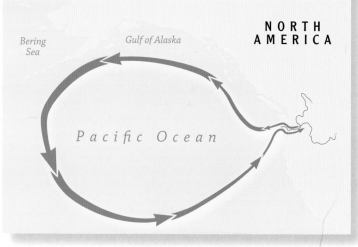

← Salmon migration route

Arctic Ocean

ASIA

Bering Sea

Gulf of Alaska

NORTH AMERICA

Pacific Ocean

Salmon migrate between the ocean and rivers.

When the eggs hatch, the young salmon swim down the river into the ocean. There, they eat and grow. When they become adults, they migrate back to the river where they were born. They lay eggs of their own, and the cycle continues.

Other kinds of migrations

Some fish stay in fresh water or salt water when they migrate. For example, mackerel must stay in salt water. They live in the open ocean and migrate close to shore to lay their eggs.

Freshwater fish migrate for reasons other than laying eggs. For example, bass and perch live in lakes. During summer, they stay near the surface. But in the winter, the surface of the lake freezes over. These fish then migrate down to deeper waters.

Mackerel migrate from the open ocean to shores when it is time to lay eggs.

Where Do Fish Live?

Fish live almost anywhere there is water. Some fish live in shallow areas near the ocean's surface. Others live at the bottom of the sea. Still others live in fast-flowing rivers, or in pitch-black caves. These underwater **habitats** provide fish with the food and shelter they need to survive.

Some fish live in freshwater habitats, such as this spring.

Warm water, cold water

Most fish can only live in water that has a certain temperature range. For example, fish that live in the warm waters near tropical (warm) regions could not survive in the ice-cold waters of the Arctic Ocean. If the water temperature where they live changes too quickly, the fish will die.

Light and dark

Sunlight plays an important role in fish habitats. Surface waters or shallow areas get lots of sunlight, so many plants or plantlike living things can grow there. These living things provide a source of food for fish and other animals.

The strange fish of the deep sea are adapted for life in cold, pitch-black water.

Sunlight is important in fish habitats. Underwater areas with lots of sunlight can usually support more life.

Light from the sun only reaches the upper layers of water. The deepest parts of the ocean and deep lakes are totally black. They don't have the plants and other tiny living things found at surface waters, so deep-sea fish and other animals have to find other sources of food.

Salt water and fresh water

The salinity (saltiness) of water also affects where fish live. The water of the ocean is salty. But lakes and rivers have fresh water. Only a few kinds of fish, such as salmon, can move between salt water and fresh water.

Some fish are **adapted** for living in water that is both salty and fresh. This water is found at the mouths of rivers that flow into oceans.

Fun Fact

Fish breathe oxygen in the water with their **gills.** Some water has more oxygen than other water. This can determine where certain fish can live.

What Fish Live Near Ocean Shores?

Oceans provide many different **habitats** for fish, including several near ocean shores. The water near seashores is shallow and sunlit, so many plants and plantlike living things grow there. Ocean shores support huge numbers of animals—including many kinds of fish.

The fierce-looking wolffish hides in rocky crevices near shores.

Kelp forests grow in cold waters close to shore. They are home to many fish.

Shallow seas

Many fish live in the warm, shallow seas surrounding continents and islands. Small fish like anchovies travel together in **schools** and provide food for larger fish. **Predators** like hammerhead sharks and great white sharks are also found in warm waters.

Many shoreline fish have **adaptations** to help them hunt for food. Doctorfish use their small, sharp teeth to scrape plantlike **algae** from sand and rocks. They often eat in schools, much like herds of cows grazing grass.

Kelp forests

Kelp is a kind of seaweed. Like plants, it gets energy from sunlight. Along colder ocean shores, kelp grows as tall as trees. Large groups of kelp form beautiful underwater forests.

Some kinds of fish are specially adapted for living in kelp forests. Kelpfish have long, blade-shaped bodies that look like the leaves of kelp. This **camouflage** helps hide them from predators. Some kelpfish can even change colors to better blend in with kelp.

Mangrove forests

Mangroves are trees that grow along tropical shores. Their twisty roots look somewhat like stilts sticking up from the water surface. The roots help hold the muddy shores in place. Fish and other animals swim in the water between the mangrove roots.

Fun Fact

The mudskipper is a strange fish that lives in mangrove forests. It can breathe outside of the water. Mudskippers can even climb up the branches of mangrove trees!

Mangrove trees have roots that grow underwater. The roots provide shelter for fish.

What Fish Live in Coral Reefs?

Coral reefs are some of the most colorful and beautiful places on Earth. These rocky environments are like underwater cities. They are home to a huge number of living things—including many **species** of fish. Only rain forests support more kinds of animals.

Reef builders

The rocky structures of coral reefs are built by animals called corals. Corals are squishy creatures related to jellyfish. Their bodies produce the limestone rock that makes up the reef. Most corals only live near the surface of bright, tropical waters.

Hide and seek

Coral reefs form mazes of holes and nooks. Many fish live in these hiding places. Moray eels have long, thin bodies that fit into narrow cracks. When a smaller fish or other animal passes by, the eel darts out of its hiding place and strikes at the animal.

Leafy seadragons and pipefish can hide in plain sight. They are experts at **camouflage.** So is the strange-looking frogfish. Frogfish bodies have colorful growths that look just like sponges or coral. Smaller fish cannot tell the difference, so they swim close to the frogfish's mouth—and are quickly gobbled up.

Many coral reef fish are brightly colored, which can also help them hide. Some, like the butterflyfish, have

Moray eels hide in holes and crevices in the reef. They dart out to snatch passing **prey.**

Colorful coral reefs are home to huge numbers of fish and other animals.

Frogfish use their fins to walk along sponges and coral reefs. Their bloblike bodies blend right in.

markings on their tails that look like eyes. These markings confuse **predators** and make it easier for the fish to escape.

Friendly fish

Some fish in coral reefs help each other. Small, cigar-shaped fish called wrasse often live with larger fish. The large fish sometimes have harmful **parasites** living on their bodies. The wrasse eats the parasites off the big fish's body, helping to clean it.

A small wrasse cleans around the mouth of a much larger triggerfish. The triggerfish does not eat the helpful wrasse.

What Fish Live in the Open Ocean?

Ocean shores provide food for many fish and other animals. But most of the ocean is far from land and does not support much life. These parts of the ocean are called open ocean. In some ways, they are similar to deserts on land.

Only a few kinds of fish live in the open ocean all the time. Some fish **migrate** between the open ocean and shores.

Marlin are fast swimmers. They use their swordlike jaws as weapons.

Big fish

The largest fish of all live in the open ocean. They include marlin, tuna, and sharks. These fish are protected from **predators** by their size. Few animals are big enough to eat them. Some marlins can weigh over 1,500 pounds (680 kilograms)!

Marlin, sailfish, swordfish, and other fish of the open ocean have long, pointy jaws. They use these jaws to stun animals before eating them.

Some sharks that live in the open ocean have a crescent-shaped tail that provides power for swimming.

Tuna have dark backs and silvery sides and bellies. Their coloring blends into the water.

Fast fish

Fish of the open ocean are powerful swimmers. They have to swim fast to move across the great distances of the open ocean. Their speed helps them catch other fish to eat.

The flyingfish has an unusual **adaptation** to escape big predators. Its fins act like wings. It can leap out of the water and soar through the air for 1,000 feet (300 meters)!

Hiding in plain sight

Many fish that live in the open ocean are **camouflaged** by their color. Tuna and mackerel usually have dark blue or green backs with silvery sides and bellies. They are difficult for predators to see from any angle.

Fun Fact

Oarfish are the longest bony fish, measuring 16 to 35 feet (5 to 11 meters). They live deep beneath the surface of the open ocean. Sometimes they come up to the surface. These snakelike fish may have given people the idea for legends about "sea serpents."

What Fish Live in the Deep Ocean?

The deep ocean is the largest part of Earth. It is also the most mysterious. It is a pitch-black, ice-cold world. The pressure in the deep can crush a human being.

Many strange fish live in this **habitat**. They have special **adaptations** that help them survive in the depths.

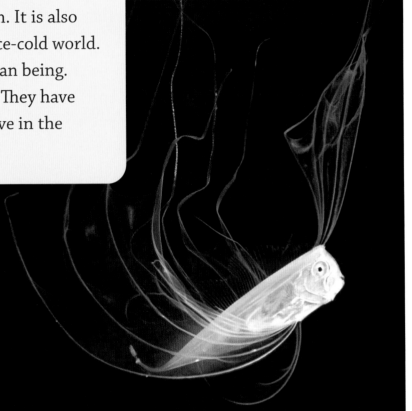

Many strange fish live in the deep sea. This young ribbon-fish has long, ghostly fins.

The better to see you

Deep-sea fish often have small bodies with huge heads and eyes. Their big eyes help them find other animals to eat. Even though the deep sea is dark, some living things produce glowing lights from their bodies, like fireflies do.

Squishy fish

To survive the crushing pressure of the deep, many fish have jellylike skin. Their squishy skin acts like cushioning, protecting them against the pressure.

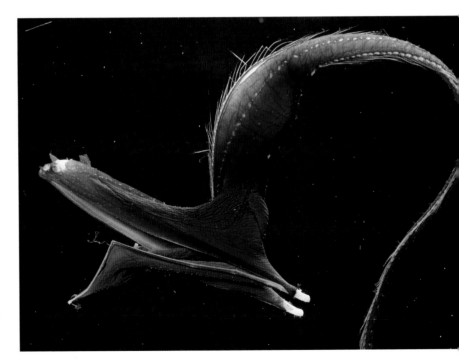

The gulper has a gigantic mouth that opens wide. It can swallow animals bigger than itself!

Sea beasts

Some deep-sea fish look like horrifying monsters. The mouth of the viperfish is filled with huge fangs. The bodies of gulper eels and black swallowers are almost all mouth. They can swallow fish bigger than they are!

But you shouldn't be too scared of these creatures. Most fish of the deep are small and slow moving. They usually drift along with the currents. Some fish, like the tripod fish, can barely swim at all. This fish uses its tail and two fins like legs to walk along the sea floor.

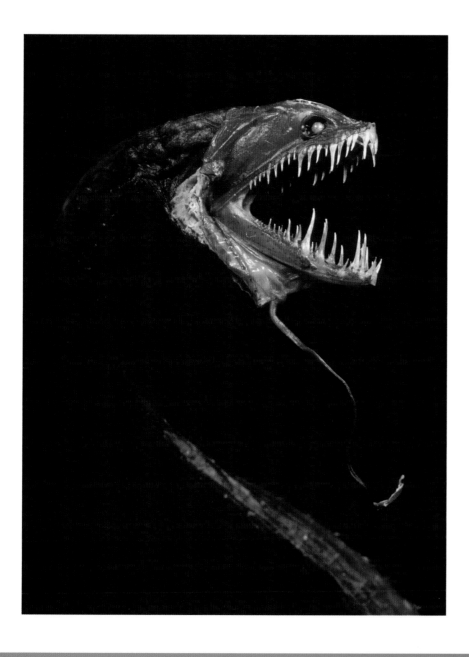

The dragonfish has pointy teeth. Like the anglerfish, it has a glowing body part that acts like a fishing lure.

What Fish Live in Lakes and Ponds?

Lakes and ponds are bodies of fresh water filled with many kinds of fish. Fish found here are often different from the ones that live in salty ocean **habitats.**

Lakes

Lakes can differ greatly in size. Some are so big and deep you can't see across them or swim to the bottom. Others are more like large ponds. But no matter what their size, lakes can provide many different habitats for fish.

Some lake fish, like trout and perch, live in shallower waters along the shores, where **algae** and plants are plentiful. Insects and other living things eat the algae and plants. They provide a tasty meal for shore-dwelling fish like minnows and other fish.

Catfish live in lakes in many parts of the world. They use whiskerlike growths around their mouths to search for food along the bottom of the lake. Catfish and other bottom-dwelling fish are often dark in color to blend in with their surroundings.

Catfish use their whiskerlike growths to feel for food along the bottom of lakes.

Ponds are often filled with plants and insects that provide food for fish like this trout.

Ponds

Ponds can be quite small and shallow. Sunlight often reaches the bottom of ponds. Because of this, plants can grow in ponds from shore to shore.

The **food chain** in ponds is similar to those found near the shorelines and shallow areas of lakes. Leafy plants often float on the surface of ponds. These plants provide food for insects and other small animals. These animals, in turn, provide food for fish like bass and catfish.

Fun Fact

Lake Victoria, in Africa, is home to over 500 kinds of a colorful fish called cichlid. These fish are found nowhere else in the world. Cichlids have **adapted** their colors to the area of the lake in which they live. **Species** that live close to the surface are often dark blue. Species that live near the bottom of the lake often come in shades of bright red.

What Fish Live in Rivers and Caves?

Rivers are long, narrow bodies of fresh water that crisscross the land. Flowing rivers can carve canyons and channels out of solid rock. Sometimes, rivers carve out underground caves and form pools of water there. The fish that live in rivers and caves are specially **adapted** to these environments.

Piranhas are fierce fish of the Amazon River. Their sharp teeth can tear apart large animals in minutes.

Rivers

Some rivers are gentle streams. Others are rushing rapids. Still others, such as the Amazon and Mississippi rivers, are huge bodies of water. They are home to many unique kinds of fish.

Piranhas are a famous fish of the Amazon River. These fierce fish have razor-sharp teeth. A **school** of piranhas can tear apart a large animal in minutes!

The paddlefish is a strange fish of the Mississippi River. Its long mouth is shaped like a paddle. Scientists think the paddlefish uses its "paddle" to sense for food.

Salmon come to rivers to lay their eggs. The rocks along river bottoms provide good shelter for the eggs.

Caves

Many fish that live in cave rivers and pools have ghostly pale skin and tiny eyes. Some cave fish, such as the blindfish, have no eyes at all. Eyes would be of no use to these fish anyway, because they live in total darkness.

The paddlefish lives in the Mississippi River. Scientists think it uses its long nose to sense for food.

The blind cave fish is adapted for a life in darkness. It has no eyes, which would be useless in caves.

Fun Fact

The cave angelfish lives only in the waterfalls of caves. It waits for tiny living things to flow down the waterfall and then swallows them up!

Why Are Some Fish Endangered?

You may have heard the saying, "there are plenty of fish in the sea," but this is no longer true. Some kinds of fish are **endangered.** Their numbers are so low that they could die off completely. Many human activities have endangered fish.

Fishing has killed off many fish in the ocean. Some kinds of fish could die off completely.

Overfishing

Fish is an important part of people's diet in many parts of the world. To catch enough fish to meet the demand, **commercial fishermen** often use giant nets to scoop up hundreds of fish at a time.

Overfishing not only hurts the kind of fish being caught for food. It also hurts other fish and animals, which can get caught in the fishing nets and die. Huge fishing nets also harm important ocean **habitats,** like coral reefs. They drag across the ocean floor, destroying underwater shelters that fish depend on.

The sad story of sharks

People are often afraid of sharks, but they are an important part of the ocean **food chain.** They eat many kinds of fish and help control their numbers. Today, some **species** of shark are endangered.

Sharks are in danger because people hunt them for their fins. Cooks use the fins to make a special soup.

Many fishermen catch and kill sharks for their fins, which are used to make a special soup. Shark fin soup has become very popular in some parts of the world, and fishermen get paid a lot of money for shark fins. Sharks are being killed in great numbers. Many people worry that they will never recover.

Pollution

Pollution can also cause harm to fish. Pollution includes garbage, chemicals, and other wastes caused by human activities. Oil spills in the ocean kill many fish. Factories release waste into rivers and lakes, poisoning fish there. Even clean water from factories can harm fish. Such water is often hotter than the water in the rivers or lakes. The fish cannot adjust to the warmer temperature and may die.

Pollution from oil spills can destroy shore habitats, causing much harm to the fish that live there.

How Can We Protect Fish?

There are many ways that people can help protect fish. Some governments, organizations, and individuals are working to help keep fish and their **habitats** healthy. Each of us can do our part to help.

Making laws

Some countries have made laws that stop people from fishing in certain areas. They have also made laws that limit the amount of **pollution** that can be dumped into bodies of water. Other laws limit fishing activities so that only certain kinds of fish are allowed to be caught during certain times of the year. By limiting fishing in this way, fishermen can catch food for people while allowing the numbers of fish to recover.

Fishing limits can protect fish while allowing some fishing.

Raising fish on fish farms means less fish need to be caught in the ocean.

Hatcheries and fish farms

Certain kinds of fish, like salmon, can be bred and raised by people. After a certain amount of time, these fish can be released into the wild. Once they are in their natural habitat, their numbers may recover.

Some fish can also be bred and raised on "farms" offshore. By raising fish in this way, people do not need to catch as many wild fish. But fish farms must be carefully controlled. Waste from fish farms can release pollution into nearby bodies of water.

Education

Another way to help fish is to raise awareness and educate people about them. For example, some people think sharks are "bad" animals and might not care if they are **endangered.** But sharks, like other fish, are an important part of the environment. By studying these fascinating creatures, we can learn more about ways to protect them.

Scientists can learn much from studying fish, including sharks.

Activities

Fish Habitats

Introduction: Fish **habitats** are some of the most amazing places on Earth. You can find out more about these places—and the fish and other creatures that live there—by looking up information about them in your school or public library.

Materials:

• Poster board • Markers

Directions:

1. Choose a fish habitat that you'd like to learn more about. You may wish to choose habitats that appear in this book, like wetlands, coral reefs, kelp forests, mangroves, or the deep ocean.

2. Ask your teacher, family member, or school or public librarian to help you look up information about this habitat. You may wish to write down a list of questions you have about this habitat. Examples of such questions include:

   • Where in the world is this habitat found?

   • What kinds of plants, fish, and other animals live there?

   • What kinds of **adaptations** do animals have to living in this habitat?

   • What are threats facing this habitat?

   • What are people doing to protect this habitat?

3. Draw a picture of your chosen habitat. Be sure to label its main features, including some of the plants and animals that live there. Present your poster to your class or to family and friends.

Endangered Fish Research Project

Introduction: Many kinds of fish are **endangered** because of human activities or other causes. We can help protect endangered animals by telling people about the threats to these animals.

You can find out more about endangered fish in your region or country by looking up information in your school or public library.

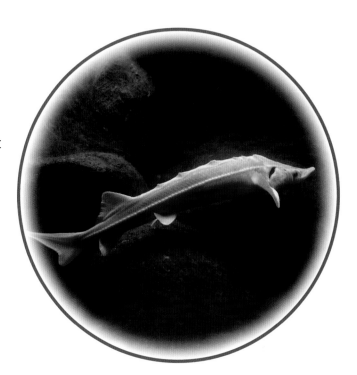

The white sturgeon is an endangered fish of North America.

Materials:

• Poster board • Markers

Directions:

1. Ask a family member, teacher, or your school or public librarian to help you find information on endangered fish in your region or country.

2. Choose a fish that you wish to learn more about. Write down important information about the fish and why it is endangered. Questions you may wish to answer include:

    • What region of the world does this fish live in?

    • What is unique about the fish?

    • What is the fish's natural habitat?

    • How long has the fish been endangered?

    • What are people doing to help protect the fish?

3. Draw a picture of the fish on the poster board. Write down information about the fish you'd like to share with others. You can present what you found out to your class, family, or friends.

Glossary

adaptation; adapted a feature or trait that helps a living thing survive in its environment; fitted.

algae a group of simple, plantlike living things.

camouflage (n.) special coloring or texture that helps an animal blend in with its environment; (v.) to look like something else in order to hide.

cartilage a rubbery tissue that makes up the skeletons of some animals.

cold-blooded having blood that is about the same temperature as the air or water around the animal.

commercial fisherman a fisherman who catches large amounts of fish with nets and sells them.

endangered in danger of dying off completely.

fertilize to make a thing start to grow.

food chain a system linking animals, the things they eat, and the things that eat them.

gill the body part that a fish, tadpole, crab, or other water animal uses to breathe in water.

habitat a place where a plant or animal lives in the wild.

larva; larvae a young version of an animal; more than one larva.

lateral line a system of channels under a fish's skin that helps it sense the motion of water.

life cycle the stages of development that a living thing passes through.

migrate; migration to move from one region to another; the movement of animals to a place that offers better living conditions.

parasite an animal or other living thing that lives off another living thing's body.

pollution all the ways that human activity harms nature.

predator a hunting animal.

prey any animal or animals hunted for food by another animal.

school a group of fish that swims close together.

species a group of animals or plants that have certain permanent characteristics in common and are able to breed with one another.

swim bladder a body part in fish that fills with gas, allowing the fish to float in water.

vertebrate an animal with a backbone.

Find Out More

Books

The Fish Classes by Rebecca Stefoff (Benchmark Books, 2008)

Five classes of fish are described by their physical features, habitats, ways of life, and factors threatening their future.

Incredible Fish by John Townsend (Raintree, 2005)

This book first describes what are the normal characteristics of fish, then introduces you to weird fish that are not normal.

The Life Cycle of Fish by Louise and Richard Spilsbury (Heinemann Library, 2003)

The emphasis in this book is on the life processes of fish and the environment they live in.

Underwater World by Deborah Coldiron (ABDO Publishing, 2007-2008) multivolume set

Each title in this series describes one species of fish and discusses the environmental threats it faces.

Web sites

Bony Fishes

http://www.seaworld.org/infobooks/BonyFish/home.html

Sea World (located in California, Florida, and Texas) has assembled a number of fact sheets on bony fish, including habitat and distribution, senses, eating habits, and conservation.

FishFAQ

http://www.nefsc.noaa.gov/faq/index.html

Woods Hole Science Aquarium answers tons of questions about fish, for example, "Do fish sleep?" "What is chitin?" and "Can fish swim backwards?"

Ichthyology: Just for Kids

http://www.flmnh.ufl.edu/fish/kids/kids.htm

The Florida Museum of Natural History explains how fish adapt to their surroundings, how they swim, and how to avoid a shark attack.

National Geographic Kids: Animals Creature Features

http://kids.nationalgeographic.com/Animals/CreatureFeature

Click on "Fish" in the menu to learn about the bull shark, clown anemonefish, great white shark, hammerhead shark, mola, sand tiger shark, and stingray.

U.S. Fish & Wildlife Service: Kids' Corner

http://www.fws.gov/endangered/kids/

The focus is on how you can get involved in saving our wildlife and conserving their natural habitats.

Index